STRATEGIES FOR SUCCESS
in Writing

PREPARATORY LEVEL

June Coultas, Ed. D. and James Swalm, Ed. D.

STRATEGIES FOR SUCCESS *in Writing*
P R E P A R A T O R Y   L E V E L

Table of Contents

Introduction

We think of the writers of books as wonderful and mysterious people. But, this isn't so. Writers are real people. They're just like us, with one difference.

Writers have put their words on paper for us to read and to enjoy. Without writers, there wouldn't be anything for us to read. However, we can be writers, too. We have stories to tell, adventures to share, and information to give.

In this book, we will learn more about being writers. We will have chances to write different things. Being a good writer just takes some time, some patience, and some practice.

Our society cannot work well if people cannot read, write, or do math. Testing is one way that you can find out how well you are learning these skills.

The material in this book has been carefully prepared to help you learn the skills you will see on writing tests. You will become aware of your strengths and weaknesses. Then you can practice the skills that give you trouble.

This book also provides you with test-taking strategies. You will have that extra edge you need to do well on tests.

This text will give you the tools to succeed. We wish you well!

UNIT 1: Prewriting Strategies

CHAPTER ONE: GETTING STARTED

There are times when you will be told what you should write about. At other times, you will be asked to come up with your own ideas. However, whether you are a beginning or an experienced writer, there are times when it is difficult to get started. You need to get your thoughts organized.

This planning is a very important step that all good writers take. This is called *prewriting*, meaning "what you do before you write."

In the prewriting stage, ask yourself some questions.

- *Who will read what I'm writing? Is it just for the teacher or will others read it?*

- *Do I have to write on a certain topic? Can I write about anything I choose?*

- *What type of writing do I have to do? Will I write a story, a report, a letter, or a description of something?*

These are important first questions. Your answers will help you to understand **who the audience is**, **what the topic is**, and **what form the writing will take**.

Your Audience

Who is your audience? As you plan your writing, you have to know who will be reading what you have written. You want your writing to be of interest to your readers.

You can divide your readers into three kinds of audiences:

      1 **People You Know Very Well**

      2 **People You Know a Little**

      3 **People You Don't Know**

Think of categories of people you know. **Your family** and **your friends** are two examples. Authors need to think about their audience. It can make a difference in the way they say things. It can even make a difference in the topics and the type of writing they do.

Your Turn 1

> Who are your audiences? Make three lists. Don't use actual names of people. Use categories.

People You Know Well	People You Know a Little	People You Don't Know
1. family	1. neighbors	1. the mayor
2.	2.	2.
3.	3.	3.
4.	4.	4.
5. others	5. others	5. others

> Explain how some people could appear on more than one list.

> Compare your lists with the lists of your classmates. Are they similar? Did your friends suggest groups of people that were different from yours? You may want to add other groups to your lists.

Your Turn 2

> Discuss with your classmates how your writing might be different if you were writing to a favorite relative or if you were writing to the President of the United States.

Writing Topics

Your topics can be grouped into one of three general headings:

        1 **Specific Topics**
        2 **General Topics**
        3 **Personal Choice Topics**

1 Example of a Specific Topic

Write a report about the African elephant becoming an endangered species. Tell where it lives. Tell why it is in danger of becoming extinct. Tell what is being done or should be done to save it.

This assignment asks you to write a report about a specific animal. The report must include a number of details about that animal.

2 Example of a General Topic

Write a report about an animal that is considered an endangered species.
This assignment offers you a choice. You can write a report about any endangered species.

3 Example of a Personal Choice Topic

Write a story about a real or imaginary animal you would like for a pet.
This assignment gives you the greatest choice. You can write a story about any animal you want, even one you make up.

✎ Your Turn 3

● ●

> With a partner, make three lists of writing topics for each of the topic types: a *specific topic*, a *general topic*, and a *personal choice topic*. Choose topics that you would like to write about.

> Share your topics with the class. See if they agree that your topics fit the types. If not, rewrite them to make them fit.

Different Forms of Writing

Once you know your audience and your topic, you need to think about what form your writing should take.

There are different forms of writing. Each of them can be used for different purposes. Three of the most common forms are the **story**, the **letter**, and the **report**. Many different kinds of writing are based on these three forms. In this section, we will discuss these three basic forms of writing.

A. Writing a Story

What belongs in a story?

✔ **A story has a theme or main idea.** The theme answers the question: "What was the story about?"

✔ **A story has a character or characters.** Characters can be humans, animals, or imaginary people.

✔ **A story has a setting.** The setting tells us when and where the story takes place. The "when" can be in the past, the present, or in the future. It can be a season, a day, or an hour.

✔ **A story has a plot.** The plot is what happens. It is made up of events that lead to the solution of some kind of a problem.

STORY FORM

THEME (MAIN IDEA)		
CHARACTERS (people/ animals)	**SETTING** (when and where the story takes place)	**PLOT** (what happens in the story)

✎ **Your Turn 4**

● ●

> ❯ Make a chart like the one on the bottom of the previous page.

> ❯ Using a story you have read, fill in the boxes with the main idea, the names of the characters, the setting, and the plot.

> ❯ Using the information on the paper you just filled in, write at least one sentence describing one of the characters.

> ❯ Write another sentence telling when and where the story takes place (setting).

> ❯ Next, tell about one important event in the story. Write about what caused the event, and what happened as a result of it.

> ❯ Write three final sentences:

> > ① **one telling the problem**
> > ② **one telling how the problem was solved**
> > ③ **one telling the theme or main idea of the story**

B. Writing a Letter

There are two different types of letters. One is a *friendly letter*, which you write to friends and relatives. In this letter, you tell the person who will read the letter about personal matters. These might include what you have been doing or what is new in your life. The other is a *business letter*. This is a more formal type of letter. It is written to someone who is not a friend or relative. It may be about a matter you think is important for that person to know.

Often you write business letters when you need help in solving a problem. Sometimes you will write this kind of letter to tell your opinion about something. You may want to convince someone that you are right. In this case, a business letter is the best kind of letter to use.

Friendly Letter

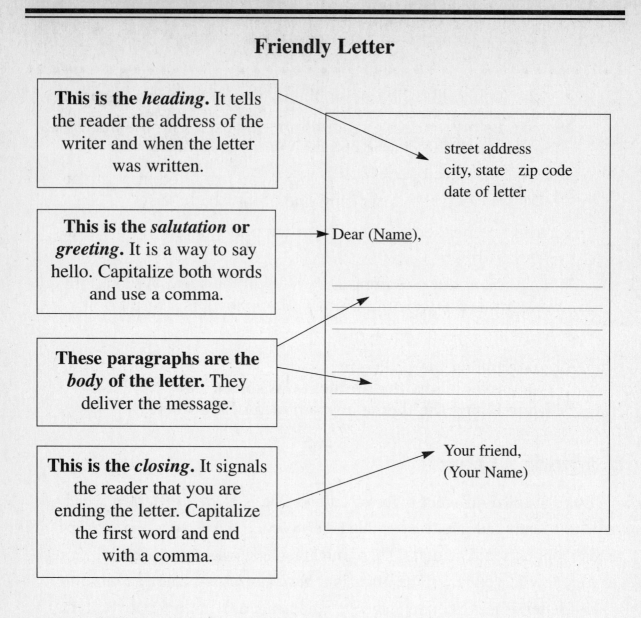

This is the *heading*. It tells the reader the address of the writer and when the letter was written.

This is the *salutation* or *greeting*. It is a way to say hello. Capitalize both words and use a comma.

These paragraphs are the *body* of the letter. They deliver the message.

This is the *closing*. It signals the reader that you are ending the letter. Capitalize the first word and end with a comma.

street address
city, state   zip code
date of letter

Dear (Name),

Your friend,
(Your Name)

✍ Your Turn 5

• •

> You have been given a pair of in-line skates for your birthday. Write a personal letter to a friend or relative. Tell him/her about the skates. Say how much you are enjoying them. The letter could also tell about some of the things that you did when you used the skates.

Business Letter

There are some differences between the business letter and the friendly letter. The business letter also includes a **heading**, a **salutation** or **greeting**, the **body**, and a **closing**. Unlike a friendly letter, a business letter includes an **inside address**. The inside address gives the person's name and address. An example of an inside address is:

Mr. Wilson Tuttle, Sales Manager
Western Sporting Goods Company
5609 North Canal Street
Chicago, IL 66780

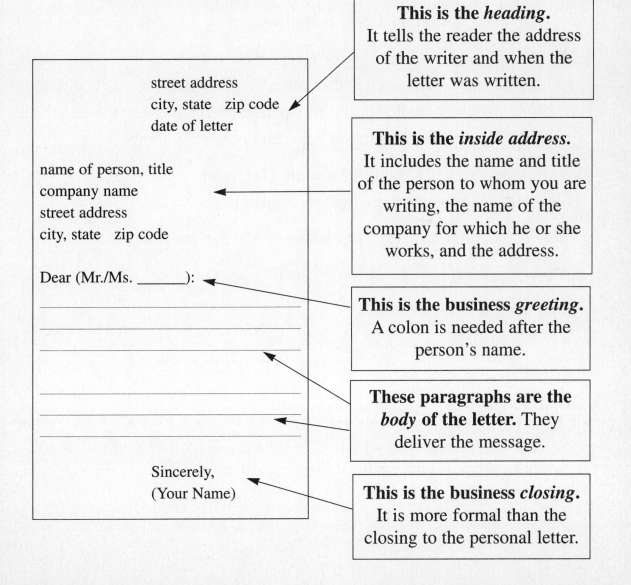

street address
city, state   zip code
date of letter

This is the *heading*.
It tells the reader the address of the writer and when the letter was written.

name of person, title
company name
street address
city, state   zip code

This is the *inside address*.
It includes the name and title of the person to whom you are writing, the name of the company for which he or she works, and the address.

Dear (Mr./Ms. _____):

This is the business *greeting*.
A colon is needed after the person's name.

These paragraphs are the *body* of the letter. They deliver the message.

Sincerely,
(Your Name)

This is the business *closing*.
It is more formal than the closing to the personal letter.

C. Writing a Report

A report is designed to present facts in an organized way. You might think of it as a factual type of story.

✔ The **first paragraph** introduces the subject.

✔ The **paragraphs that follow** provide information about the subject.

✔ The **final paragraph** summarizes the report.

Let's suppose that you were asked to write reports on the following topics:

> ❯ *Explain why you think it is important to be careful when you are riding a bicycle.*

> ❯ *Write three reasons why people should not throw paper, cans, and other litter on the streets.*

Each of these assignments asks for a report on a specific topic. The exact length of each report may not be the same. Reports can be many different lengths. Some may be completed in a few paragraphs. Other reports may take several pages. The length of the report depends upon many things.

Factors that affect the length of a report include:

1 the amount of research the writer chooses to do

2 the amount of knowledge of and interest in the topic the writer has

3 the topic itself

4 the type of audience

5 the purpose of the report

✍ Your Turn 6

• •

> ❯ Write a report telling why it is or is not important for students to stay in school. Give at least three reasons.

Other Forms of Writing

There are many other forms of writing. Some are:

POEMS

PLAYS

ADVERTISEMENTS

ADVICE COLUMNS

Even instructions about how to do something are a form of writing. You will learn about some of these other types of writing later in the book. Before you continue, try the activity below.

✍ Your Turn 7

● ●

> ➤ How could you make the world a better place in which to live? Write your response to this question. You may choose one of the three basic forms of writing that you learned about in this chapter (**story**, **letter**, or **report**).

CHAPTER TWO: GETTING ORGANIZED

Once you have decided who your audience is, what your topic will be, and what form your writing should take, the next step is preparing to write. This is the time when you must think about what you will say in your writing.

Unfortunately, many beginning writers start writing almost as soon as they are told what the topic is. You need to take some time to think about the topic. You need to plan what you wish to say to your audience.

Writers need to examine what they know about a topic. Then, they can decide the best way to write about it. Planning how to present what you want to write is called **organizing**.

In this chapter, we will explore some strategies that will help you organize a writing task. You may like some strategies more than others. But, you should try to pick the strategy that would be most helpful for each task.

Order of Events

In many types of writing, it is important to place ideas or events in the correct order. This is called **sequential order**. A *sequence* is a series of things that follow each other in logical order. One kind of sequential order is **chronological order**. This means that events are written in the order that they happened. We often write about history in chronological order. This makes it easier to understand.

In the following example, you can see how chronological order works. One event follows another in the order that each event happened.

1. *English-speaking people became concerned about their religious freedom.*

2. *They decided to come to the New World.*

3. *They sailed to America on the ship called the Mayflower.*

4. *They landed at a place they called Plymouth.*

5. *Plymouth Rock marks their landing.*

6. *Many people died.*

7. *Survivors and Native Americans gathered food for a harvest feast.*

8. *This became the traditional holiday known as Thanksgiving.*

✍ Your Turn 1

● ●

> ➤ Here are some events in the life of Abraham Lincoln. Put them in the correct *chronological order*. The first event is done for you.

A Abraham Lincoln grew up in Indiana. _____

B Abraham Lincoln was assassinated in April 1865. _____

C Abraham Lincoln and his family lived in Springfield, Illinois, when he ran for president. _____

D Abraham Lincoln became president in 1860. _____

E Abraham Lincoln was born in Kentucky in 1809. **1st**

F Abraham Lincoln, his wife, and three of their sons were buried in Springfield, Illinois. _____

> ➤ You may not know the correct order in which the events in President Lincoln's life took place. But, you can put the events into a logical order.

Sequential order does not have to involve historical events. It can also be used to organize everyday tasks, or the steps needed to complete a project. For example, suppose you wanted to tell someone how to make an ice cream soda. You might organize the steps in this order:

How to Make an Ice Cream Soda

1. *Place two tablespoons of chocolate syrup into a big glass.*

2. *Add a little milk.*

3. *Fill the glass with club soda. Stir the soda as you pour.*

4. *Put in one scoop of ice cream.*

✍ Your Turn 2

• •

➤ Let's try a simple exercise. Describe how you would make a bed with fresh sheets. This is a *sequential* task. How would you organize these steps? Do you think everyone would do it the same way?

➤ Decide the order in which you would do each step.

A Smooth the bedspread or comforter. _____

B Place the bottom sheet on the bed. _____

C Tuck in the blanket and the top sheet. _____

D Take the sheets off the bed. _____

E Put the pillow cases on the pillows. _____

F Get the sheets from the closet. _____

G Place the top sheet on the bed. _____

The two exercises that you did show how you can organize items in a logical order. If you were writing a report, you would explain these events or tasks in greater detail. Each of them would become part of a paragraph. The paragraph would be made up of sentences giving details about the events or tasks.

Putting events in order is also a way of organizing story writing. Many stories are written in chronological order.

1. After the beginning, a **problem** occurs.
2. Then there is a series of **events** that lead to a **solution**.
3. After the problem is **solved**, there is an **ending**.

Story Model

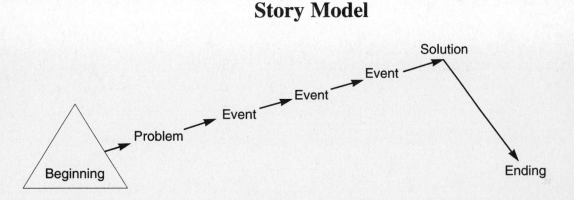

Think of the story of Cinderella. How does it fit this organizational model?

✍ Your Turn 3

• •

➤ Use a story that you know. List the events that take place in the order in which they happen. Also give the solution to the story's problem. Use the model that appears above.

Remember that things happen in a story for a reason. Usually one event is the cause of the next event.

Story Map

Another way of organizing your ideas about a topic is to develop a **story map**. A story map puts the most important idea in the center of the chart. Other ideas that describe the main idea are placed around it.

Looking at a story map will help you decide what your piece of writing will contain. It can also help you organize what will be in each paragraph.

Here is an example of a story map.

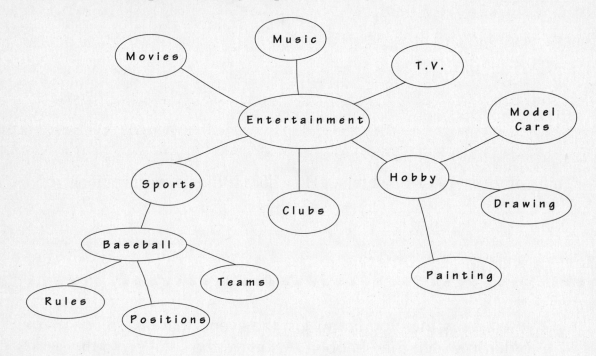

✍ Your Turn 4

> Use the story map strategy. Develop your own story map for the following topic:

★ You find a stray dog as you walk home one afternoon. It follows you home.

✔ Decide what steps you could take to find the dog's owner or home.
✔ List the events that might happen.
✔ Use your imagination!

✍ Your Turn 5

> Now write a story using your story map. Use the map to help you decide what to include in your story. Also, use the information on your map to help you create the paragraphs.

Organizing Persuasive Writing

Sometimes you think differently about something than your friends or family. When this happens, you need to present or "argue" your point of view. You need to persuade your friends or family to agree with you. We call this kind of writing **persuasive writing**.

As always, you need to think of ways to organize your ideas before you begin to write. Organizing your ideas for this type of writing is different than organizing for other types. There are three prewriting strategies you could use to help you to plan what you want to include in this type of writing:

    A. **Comparison/Contrast Model**

    B. **Pro/Con Model**

    C. **Venn Diagram**

A. Comparison/Contrast Model

In a *comparison/contrast* model, you need to list either how things are alike or similar (comparison), or how things are different (contrast).

When you are trying to persuade someone to agree with you, you will probably want to show how your ideas or choices are better than another idea or choice. So, you will want to contrast the two sides of the problem.

Let's consider three versions of a *comparison/contrast* model.

1. Comparison

This chart tries to show how chickens and ducks are **alike**.

CHICKENS	DUCKS
a bird	a bird
has feathers	has feathers
has two legs	has two legs
hatches from eggs	hatches from eggs
may be raised for food	may be raised for food

2. Contrast

This chart tries to show how chickens and ducks are **different**.

CHICKENS	DUCKS
have feet with claws	have webbed feet
have pointed beaks	have flat bills
can't swim	can swim
crow	quack
a common farm animal	often a wild bird

3. Comparison/Contrast

This chart compares *and* contrasts chickens and ducks.

How chickens and ducks are alike	How chickens and ducks are different
• Both are hatched from eggs. • Both can be raised for food. • Both have many different species. • Both come in many colors. • Both take care of their young.	• Chickens are farm animals, but many ducks are wild. • Ducks have webbed feet for swimming; chickens have claws for walking. • They make different sounds.

✍ Your Turn 6

● ●

> ➤ *Compare and contrast* two different animals, such as lions and elephants; or two different insects, such as honey bees and wasps; or two different cities, such as New York and Los Angeles. Or, choose your own things to compare and contrast.

> ➤ Use the comparison/contrast model to list the ways that they are similar and the ways that they are different.

B. Pro/Con Model

For the *pro/con* model, picture a balance scale.

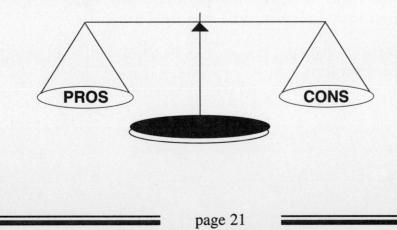

Reasons **for** something would be on one side of the scale. Reasons **against** it would be on the other side of the scale. This type of model helps you to look at a problem and arrive at a decision by "weighing" the two sides.

Let's say you were thinking about getting a dog as a pet.

Having a Dog as a Pet

PRO (For)	CON (Against)
A dog is friendly.	A dog sheds hair.
A dog can keep your home safe.	A dog needs to be walked.
A dog can be taught tricks.	A dog can chew on things.
A dog can protect children.	A dog can be expensive.

By comparing the pros and cons of a topic, a decision can be made more easily. Often writers will use this strategy to convince you that their positions are correct.

✎ Your Turn 7

> You are asked to explain why you are for or against something. Some examples might be:

- ✦ a change in the choice of lunches that are available in the cafeteria
- ✦ the clothes you must wear in a gym when exercising
- ✦ anything that you have just been told to do.

> Using a *pro/con* list, write down both the positive and negative sides of the problem.

C. Venn Diagram

A **Venn diagram** is a drawing you can make with two overlapping circles or ovals. It shows similarities and differences. When you are writing about two topics, you can see each topic's own characteristics. A Venn diagram also helps you see the characteristics the two topics share.

If you created a *Venn diagram*, it would look like this:

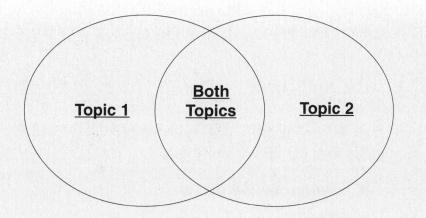

Let's suppose that two people are running for office. You like them both, but you want to vote for the one that is best for the job. You could use a *Venn diagram* to help you to decide which one to choose. It can help you to see the best traits of each candidate and the traits they share in common.

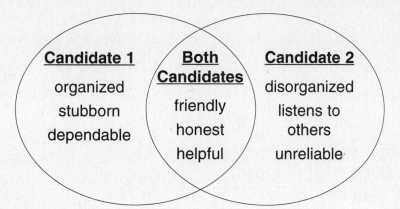

Organizing the two candidates' qualities in this way helps you make a judgment about who would be better for the job. You could use the Venn diagram to help you write about the election.

✍ Your Turn 8

> ❯ Use a Venn diagram. Compare how two items are alike and how they are different. You can choose two books, movies, or television shows, two sports or teams, or any other items that you would like to compare.

You have now learned about three types of prewriting strategies that can be used to organize ideas for persuasive writing:

- ✔ **comparison/contrast**
- ✔ **pro/con**
- ✔ **Venn diagram**

To illustrate these three ways of organizing information, we will look at the following examples.

Example 1: Comparison/Contrast Chart

You are asked to write a science report. You must explain how oak trees and pine trees are similar and how they are different. You can use a simple comparison/contrast chart that will list the ways that they are *similar on one side* and the ways that they are *different on the other*.

How oak and pine trees are similar	How oak and pine trees are different
They are both trees.	They are used for different purposes.
They can be grown in people's yards.	One grows from an acorn, and the other grows from a pine cone seed.
They provide shelter for birds.	One sheds leaves in the fall and the other keeps its needles all year.

You would probably want to add other items to each of the columns. This chart would organize your writing.

Example 2: Pro/Con Chart

Let's pretend that you are asked to write a report about whether you are in favor of or against students having the same teachers for more than one year. You can use the *pro/con chart* to organize this topic.

List the advantages of having a teacher for more than one year on the "Pro" side. You use the "Con" side to list why this is not a good idea.

Having the Same Teacher for More Than One Year

Pro	Con
The student and teacher would know each other better.	People like having different teachers.
The teacher would know what was taught last year.	Some teachers like different subjects and teach them differently.

There are other ideas that you could add. From these two lists, you would form an opinion and then write a report. You would give both sides of the topic and explain why you think your opinion is correct.

Example 3: Venn Diagram

Let's pretend that you are asked to write a letter explaining why you like one restaurant more than another. Before you write your letter, you want to organize your information by making a *Venn diagram*.

You list the things that are true only about Restaurant 1; next, list the things that are true only about Restaurant 2. In the middle, you would list things that are true about both restaurants.

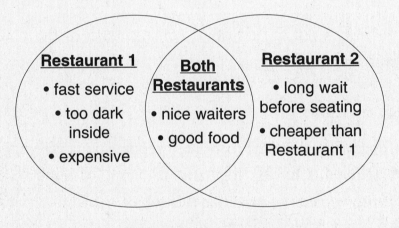

Making a List

For many kinds of writing, it is helpful to make a list of things you want to include. This strategy is very useful for keeping track of items that you want to remember. It will also help you include information in an order that makes sense.

For example, suppose you wanted to tell someone about what you did last Saturday. You would need to write down the things that you did. These events would **not** have to be listed in *chronological order*. You could organize them that way later when you write your story or letter. But, first you want to get everything on paper.

What I Did Last Saturday

★ *I began reading my new book.*

★ *I had eggs for breakfast.*

★ *I watched a baseball game on television.*

★ *I went to the store with my brother and sister.*

★ *I went to bed early.*

★ *I visited my best friend.*

★ *I took my dog for a walk.*

You could add more items to your list as you think of them. Use your list to decide what you want to include. In your writing, you can give more details about what you did.

✍ Your Turn 9

● ●

➤ Choose one of the topics below:

✔ Think of what you did yesterday. Make a list of events that you want to include. Then write paragraphs about your day.

✔ You have to write a report about your favorite movie. Make a list of the items you want to include in your report. After you finish your list, write your paragraphs.

Summary

As you have seen, there are **many different strategies** that can help you plan your writing. Often, the choice of how you organize your ideas is up to you. *There is no one right or wrong way to start.*

The purpose of using a **prewriting strategy** is simply to give you a way to put your ideas together. It will help you to write better.

This chapter has presented strategies on how to organize your ideas before you write. In the next chapter, you will be asked to write. However, before you begin your writing, always use one of the prewriting strategies you learned in this chapter. In this way, your writing will be better organized. It will be easier to read and understand.

UNIT 2: Types of Writing

CHAPTER THREE: THE FOUR KINDS OF TEXT

In the first two chapters, you learned about the different people for whom you might be writing. You also learned some organizational strategies to use before your write.

Now you will do some actual writing. You will produce what is called a **first draft**. A first draft is your first try at writing something. Your writing will not be perfect. There will be changes and corrections that you have to make before you can share your writing with your audience.

One of the problems beginning writers have is that once they write something, they think it is finished. This usually is not so. Experienced writers change what they write. They check for errors in spelling, punctuation, grammar, and organization. They want to be sure that their work is free of errors. They want to be sure their writing says what they wish the reader to know. This is called **revising and editing**.

In the next chapter, we will help you learn how to *revise* and *edit* your work. But for now, we would just like you to write. After you are finished writing, you should share your work with your classmates. Ask them if they have suggestions on how you might improve it or make it more interesting.

If you think your classmates' ideas will improve your writing, consider how you might change parts of your work. But remember, you are the author. You have to be pleased with your writing. If you feel someone's advice changes what you are trying to say, you do not need to take the advice.

There are four types of writing that you will be asked to try in this chapter. They are the following:

1. **Narrative Text**
2. **Informational Text**
3. **Persuasive Text**
4. **Everyday/Work Text**

Narrative Text

As we learned in Chapter 1, the story is one of the basic forms of writing. In narrative writing, you are telling a story. This doesn't mean that what you are saying has to be imaginary. You can write about a made-up event, but you can also write about something that really happened. A narrative text could be about meeting a mermaid on the bottom of the ocean or it could be about something exciting you did over the weekend.

✍ Your Turn 1

➤ A children's magazine has asked its readers for stories. You want to send in a story to be published.

➤ You decide to write about an adventure in an imaginary country. Use the story form on page 8 to help you jot down ideas for:

★ the theme
★ the characters
★ the setting
★ the plot

➤ Write your story.

➤ Remember, this is your first draft. Don't worry too much about mistakes. What you need to concentrate on is telling a good story.

✍ Your Turn 2

> ❯ Imagine that your arm is in a cast from your shoulder to your fingers. Write some stories about funny things that happened to you while your arm was in the cast. Or, write about the problems you are having.

> ❯ Think of how you can tell your story in three paragraphs:

> ★ The first paragraph might tell of how you broke your arm.

> ★ The second paragraph can tell about what you can do or have done while wearing the cast.

> ★ The third paragraph can be a summary about what you feel, what you want to do when the cast is off, or how you intend to keep this from happening again.

Some stories require you to use a **plot blueprint**. The plot blueprint is useful when you are writing a story that has a *sequence of events*. It can be used when writing a story in *chronological order*. Adventure and mystery stories, and even fairy tales, are often written in this style. You learned about this idea in the last chapter.

A plot blueprint is made up of:

1. After the beginning, a **problem** occurs.
2. Then there is a series of events that lead to a **solution**.
3. After the problem is **solved**, there is an **ending**.

If you were to draw the *plot blueprint*, it might look like the picture below. This picture is similar to the story model on page 17.

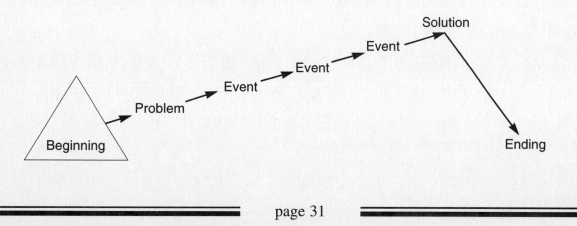

✍ Your Turn 3

> Let's pretend that you have noticed a strange car in your neighborhood for the past week. You told your family and friends about it, but they didn't think it was important. You think it is.

> Write a mystery story about what you decide to do. Tell what happens.

> Use a *story form* or a *plot blueprint* to organize your information before you write.

> Share your story with your friends. Ask them for their reaction. Were they excited? Did you keep them in suspense about what would happen? Did they have suggestions on how you might improve some part of the story?

You have now written a rough draft for three different narrative stories. In the next chapter, we will talk about how to *revise* and *edit* your writing.

Informational Text

Another type of writing deals with giving information. Informational text is the kind of writing you do when you are asked to write a **report**. A book report, a science report, or a social studies report are three kinds of informational writing that you do in school.

There may be other times when you write informational material. For example, you might be asked to write about an artist or a musician for your art or music class. You might even have to write a health report or something about a sport for physical education.

Informational writing is just what its name says it is. This type of writing gives someone information about a topic. When you do this type of writing, you often have to do research to find facts about the subject. You may need to go to the library to learn more about the subject.

If you do research, take some notes about the important facts that you wish to include in your report. You should not simply copy what you find and make that your report.

✍ Your Turn 4

> Write a report that tells who is allowed to become President of the United States.

> First, you will need to do some research. When you find the information about who can become President of the United States make a list of the key points.

> Review the key points you have written. Do you think there should be other ones? Do you think some are not needed? If so, why? This means that you need to present each point and then decide if it is needed.

✍ Your Turn 5

> Write a report about how a plant or an animal changes during its early life. You could choose a seed changing into a plant, a caterpillar changing into a butterfly, or a tadpole changing into a frog. But, you do not have to use any of these topics. You can choose anything that interests you.

> Use the *order of events* prewriting strategy. Refer to Page 14 to refresh your memory. Write down the key stages of the change before writing your report. This ensures that you tell your story in the right order.

You wrote these two reports for your teacher or your class. However, many authors write for other audiences. For instance, the authors of your science or social studies books wrote informational material for you.

When you write an informational piece, you might want to do a *story map*. This will help you to think about the topic. This will also help you to organize your thoughts. Then you will be able to write clearly.

✎ Your Turn 6

> Now try writing a report on fire safety. Pretend you are sending the report to a local newspaper to be published during Fire Prevention Week. A mapping strategy is perfect for this exercise.

> A mapping strategy will help you decide what to include in your paper. There are many things that you could include in a report about fire safety. You need to put your ideas on paper and decide what you want to include.

> After you have made your map, think of how you could write an interesting paper.

★ The first paragraph might give some general information about fire safety.

★ The paragraphs that follow could concentrate on some special things that people can do to protect themselves against fires.

★ The final paragraph could summarize what you have written. It might also give your views on how best to prevent fires.

Now that you have a better idea of how to prepare to write *informational material*, let's move on to another form of writing.

Persuasive Text

A third major type of writing is known as **persuasive** text. In this type of writing, the writer tries to get the reader to agree with him/her about something.

Where would this type of writing be found? Most often it would be found in a newspaper, a book, or a magazine. The opinion page of a newspaper is one place where this kind of text is often found.

There is another kind of persuasive writing that people do. It includes writing a **letter** to someone to try to get that person to do something. For example, if you buy a product and don't like it, you may write to the company or the store. You could ask for your money back or a different product.

Another example might be writing to a friend or a relative trying to get the person to change his or her mind about something.

✍ Your Turn 7

● ●

> You work on a newspaper. You have been asked to write an advice column that will appear in the paper.

> ★ First, pretend you are the person with a problem. Write a letter about your problem.

> ★ Then, pretend you are the advice columnist. Write a letter stating your solution to the problem.

> In this case, you might want to use the *plot blueprint* to plan your letters (See page 31). You will have a beginning, a series of events that identify the problem, and then you have a solution to the problem. It might look a little different from the narrative prewriting strategy.

✍ Your Turn 8

● ●

> Write a letter to the principal expressing your opinion for or against one of the following:

> ★ a new school rule

> ★ a class trip

> ★ a certain food served in the cafeteria

> ★ the amount of homework a teacher is giving

> When writing this letter, it is important to persuade the principal to agree with your point of view. You need to present a number of supporting details to help your position. Try to give good reasons. Simply saying you don't like something is not enough to make another person change his or her opinion.

Everyday/Work Text

This category includes the many different types of writing. It includes things that we read every day. Some examples are:

★ the road signs as you go to school

★ the advertisements on billboards

★ the signs in store windows

★ a handbook of rules

★ a form that has to be completed

★ a television guide

★ a restaurant menu

★ a program for a play or for a sporting event

★ directions of all kinds

This category of writing is completely different from *narrative*, *informational*, or *persuasive* writing. There are many different kinds of writing included in this category. There isn't one special prewriting strategy to use when you organize what you want to say. Pick the one that works best for you. Mapping or making a list are two of the most useful.

✍ Your Turn 9

● ●

> Think of a sport you play – for example, baseball, football, tennis, or swimming. Use a mapping strategy to help you organize information about the rules. Create a chart that outlines basic rules and scoring.

> Make a *map* of the things you know about the equipment used in the sport. Prepare a guide that will show how to use and care for the equipment.

You may find that these are not easy tasks. Part of the problem is that we do some things without thinking about them. We have done them so often that we don't think about how hard they are to explain to someone else.

✍ Your Turn 10

> ❯ Think about something that you do everyday or almost everyday – for example, getting dressed, eating, or brushing your teeth.

> ❯ Now, list in a sequential order how you do this task. List what you do first, second, third, and so on.

> ❯ When you are satisfied that you have included all of the steps necessary to do the task, create a sign that shows the reader how to do this task.

These kinds of writings are similar to what you might read in a set of directions, or a handbook of rules.

Now try one more example of everyday text.

✍ Your Turn 11

> ❯ Imagine that you or someone in your family wants to sell something – for example, a bicycle, a pair of skis, a car, or some furniture.

> ❯ Write an advertisement to let people know what you are selling. You might want to use a listing prewriting strategy first. Then you can be sure to include all of the important facts that will make people want to purchase the item.

We have looked at only a few of the kinds of things we read in our everyday lives. However, you now have a better idea of what it takes to write this type of material.

Summary

In this chapter you learned about four main types of writing. You used different prewriting strategies for each type. You also tried your hand at writing several selections for each of the types.

In the next chapter, we are going to look at revising and editing our writing to improve it.

UNIT 3: Revising and Editing

CHAPTER FOUR: REVISING WRITTEN MATERIAL

First drafts are not perfect. There is always room for improvement. After you finish writing a first draft, you need to read it. You need to see how it can be improved or if there are errors that need to be corrected.

- Improving the content of the writing is known as **revising**.

- Correcting technical errors, such as spelling, punctuation, and grammar is known as **editing**.

All good writers go through these two steps to make sure that their writing is as good as it can be. Good writers want their readers to understand what they are saying. They want to show that they are careful writers.

Revising

Writers can change their writing in many ways. Sometimes writers may even completely rewrite what they have written. Some of the ways you can revise your writing are:

A. **Adding information**

B. **Deleting (removing) information**

C. **Rearranging (moving) information**

D. **Combining sentences**

E. **Adding signal words and phrases**

A. Adding Information

Sometimes your writing may need more information to make it complete. After you finish writing, you may realize that you left out something. Or, maybe after some friends read what you wrote, they told you they did not understand something.

See how adding some information might improve the paragraph below.

> Some friends invited Connie to go to the beach. She told them she couldn't go. Her friend Pam was puzzled. Pam knew that Connie loved the beach. The next day, Connie called Pam and said that she would go to the beach after all.

Some questions you might ask the writer are:

★ Why did Connie say she wouldn't go to the beach?

★ What made her change her mind?

✎ Your Turn 1

➤ Revise this story by giving more information about why Connie did not want to go to the beach. Write about what made her change her mind. Decide where in the paragraph this new information should go.

B. Deleting Information

Another form of revising is to take things out of a story that don't belong. This is called **deleting information**. There are times when we include unnecessary information in our first draft. It can confuse the reader. When this occurs, the extra information should be removed.

Here is a piece of writing that contains some information that is not needed. Decide what information can be *taken out* or *deleted* so that the story is clearer.

> Terry was interested in ecology and the outdoors. Whenever he could, he went camping. Sometimes, he went with scout groups. Sometimes he went with his family.
>
> Terry liked sports. He is on the junior varsity track team.
>
> It seems that Terry has inherited his love of nature from both of his parents. His mother is a scientist who works for a company that tests water to decide if it is safe. His dad is a biology teacher in a college. They have taught Terry and and his sister to love nature.

✍ Your Turn 2

> ➤ Which of the pieces of information could be deleted without changing the story about Terry?

C. Rearranging Information

Another form of revising is **rearranging**. Rearranging means moving sentences or paragraphs to make your writing clearer. There are times when your story can be made more interesting to read by changing the order of sentences or paragraphs. This is often true of narrative writing.

Sometimes it is important to keep information in the order that it happened. This is known as *sequential order*, which you learned about in Chapter Two. It helps the reader better understand the text.

The paragraph below is an example of a narrative story that is written in *sequential order*:

> A few minutes ago, I was surprised by a large toad that hopped across my path. I fell down. I landed right in the middle of a big puddle in my driveway. Now, I am sitting down in the middle of the puddle in my shorts and T-shirt. I am all wet.

By changing the order of the story, we can make it more exciting. Sometimes only a single sentence needs to be moved to improve the organization of the writing.

A revised version of this story might look like this:

> Here I am, sitting down in the middle of a puddle in my shorts and T-shirt. A few minutes before, I was surprised by a large toad that hopped across my path. I fell down. I landed right in the middle of a big puddle in my driveway. Now I am all wet.

This revised version of the story begins in the present, then goes back to the past, and then returns to the present.

Now, let's look at a different piece of writing. This piece, a type of everyday or work text, describes how to start an herb garden. The writing is not in *sequential order*. This makes it difficult to understand.

> Put the seeds into the soil. Gently cover them with a little bit of soil.
>
> You need the right type of soil to grow your herbs. You can buy potting soil from a garden center.
>
> You can grow herbs in pots on your window sill or in a window box outside your kitchen window.

Everyday or work text is usually written in sequential order. Instructions need to show the reader each step that has to be done in order.

✍ Your Turn 3

• •

> ➤ Put the story about growing an herb garden in sequential order.

D. Combining Sentences

Another common revision is to combine two or more sentences into one better sentence. Many beginning writers use a lot of short sentences. Writing short sentences is not wrong. Yet, when there are a lot of short sentences, the writing may seem "choppy." It will not read well. By putting two or more short sentences together, you can make your writing read better.

Here are four short sentences that are all about one idea.

> Chris is lying on the sofa. He is asleep. The television is on. His science report is on the floor beside the sofa.

There are a number of ways that you could combine these ideas. You could say the same thing using fewer sentences. Let's look at some of these choices.

> Chris is stretched out on the sofa asleep. The television is on. His science report is on the floor beside the sofa.

(3 sentences)

or

> Chris is stretched out on the sofa asleep with the television on. His science report is on the floor beside the sofa.

(2 sentences)

or

> Chris is asleep with the television on and his science report on the floor beside the sofa.

(1 sentence)

✍ Your Turn 4

• •

> Below are five short sentences. Combine them into three sentences. Then try to combine them into two sentences. Finally, if you can, make one sentence out of the five sentences. Remember, it must still make sense.

> Cindy has a cat. He is black. His name is Diablo. Diablo loves to curl up inside a box. Cindy has a box in the bottom of her closet.

E. Adding Signal Words and Phrases

Have you ever noticed that sometimes your writing seems to jump from one idea to the next? There are special words that can help make your writing sound smoother. These are called *signal words* or *transition words*. They are words that send signals. They signal how one idea is connected to another idea. Think of these words as bridges connecting one part of your writing to another.

Some signal words are **when**, **then**, **next**, **after**, **at last**, **finally**, and **later**. Other signal words include **likewise**, **because**, **but**, **first**, **so**, **therefore**, **however**, **in addition**, **also**, and **as a result**.

Here is an example of a text that could be improved with the use of a signal word or phrase.

> Dee went to the movies with her friends on Saturday. Her friends loved the movie. Dee did not like it. When her friends asked her if she liked it, she told them it was good. She didn't want to hurt their feelings.

There are many ways that you could use signal words to improve the flow of the ideas in this story.

Here is an example:

> Dee went to the movies with her friends on Saturday. Her friends loved the movie. **But,** Dee did not like it. **However,** when her friends asked her if she liked it, she told them it was good. She didn't want to hurt their feelings.

✍ Your Turn 5

> Here are two paragraphs with signal words in them. Underline the signal words.

Paragraph 1

Kim wanted to go to the movies. Yet, Karen wanted to go shopping. So, the two friends had to make a decision. They agreed to go shopping first. Later they would go to the movies.

Paragraph 2

I went to a party on Saturday. First, someone spilled soda on me. Then, someone knocked a piece of birthday cake on my lap. As a result, my dress was ruined.

There are other kinds of revisions that you might make. You might move phrases to different parts of a sentence to make the writing more interesting. An example is:

> Ray and Zach went to the pizza parlor on Friday evening.

This could be changed to read:

> On Friday evening, Ray and Zach went to the pizza parlor.

or

> Ray and Zach, on Friday evening, went to the pizza parlor.

Each of the choices is correct. The only reason you might want to reorganize a sentence would be to make the story more interesting to read.

Summary

As we have seen, revising text is an important way of improving the first draft of a piece of writing. Using one or more of the revising methods listed below will help you as you work to improve your writing:

1. **add information**

2. **remove or delete information that is not needed**

3. **choose the best order for presenting information**

4. **combine sentences to form a new sentence**

5. **use signal words to connect ideas from one paragraph to the next paragraph**

6. **move phrases or the order of words in a sentence**

All of these revisions are ways of trying to improve your writing from your first draft to your final text.

CHAPTER FIVE: EDITING WRITTEN MATERIAL

Now that we have examined different ways of revising a text, we come to the editing phase of writing. When we edit, we check many things. We check to see that we have spelled words correctly. We make sure that we have used the correct punctuation. We capitalize words when needed. We make sure that we have followed the rules of good grammar and sentence structure.

Before we present our writing to audiences to read, we want to be sure that we have checked for all errors in our writing. When we have done this, we can prepare our final draft.

This chapter will discuss three of the most important things to look for when you are editing your work:

A. **Spelling**

B. **Capitalization**

C. **Punctuation**

Spelling

Let's begin our editing with attention to spelling. No one can be expected to know how to spell every word that he or she uses. All good writers check their spelling. They may use a dictionary, a spell check on their computer, or have someone else read their work. It is important to check your spelling when you are not sure. Otherwise, you may make serious mistakes.

However, you should not let concern about spelling get in the way of your writing. If you do, you will never expand your writing vocabulary. If you use the same words in your writing all the time, your writing can become dull.

Spelling Strategies

There are many ways that you can improve your spelling.

★ **One way is to make a list of words that are easy to misspell.** Many English textbooks contain such a list. If you study these words, you may remember how to spell them the next time you use them.

★ **Writing down words that you misspell is always helpful.** You can write these words in a notebook. In this way, you can build your own personal dictionary. Write the words you tend to misspell in your dictionary under the letter the word begins with. Then, when you need to use a word that you are not sure how to spell, you can look it up in your dictionary to find its proper spelling.

★ **A similar method is to use index cards to make your own dictionary.** The cards can be kept in a box with a set of alphabetical cards to separate the words.

★ **Another strategy is to read your written material backwards from the end to the beginning, from the bottom to the top of the page.** This allows you to look at the spelling of the words instead of what the words mean.

There is no way that you will know how to spell every word you might like to use. You can study the spelling rules and use the above strategies. But, remember– when in doubt, check! Only by checking the dictionary can you be sure of how a word is spelled.

✍ Your Turn 1
• •

➤ Here is a brief passage. Read it and see how many spelling errors you can find. For the purpose of this exercise, it is not necessary for you to correct the spelling mistakes. You are only to list or underline them.

Sum of my freinds lik to play diferent sports. A few of them play on the football teem, wile others are players on the basketball teem. Becuz there are only five playors necesary for basketball, a lot of us don't have enuf to do. We want the school to ofer more sports. We beleive that if this hapens, it will be good for the hole school.

Capitalization

You should only check your writing for one type of error at a time. After you have checked for spelling errors, you might check for errors in capitalization. You have had lots of practice capitalizing words. The first letter of months, countries, states, addresses, and people's names are capitalized. So, what kinds of capitalization errors should you look for?

A common error is to forget that the pronoun "I" is always a capital letter. This pronoun is used by you in place of your name. The first letter of your name is capitalized. "I" takes the place of your name, so it should also be capitalized.

We sometimes think that a title, such as *mayor* or *governor*, should be written with capital letters. This is not always true. The first letter of a title is written with a capital letter when the title appears before the name of a person. Titles are usually capitalized when used in place of a person's name. Cities, states, and countries are also capitalized.

A similar rule applies when referring to parents or relatives. You use capitals when you are using the words "Mother" or "Father" as names. These terms take the place of names. For example, you might say "You are a very good bowler, Mother." But, if you are referring to your mother not by name but as your parent, you would write: "My mother is a very good bowler."

It should not be too difficult to check your writing for errors in capitalization. Below is a brief passage. Check for capitalization errors.

✍ Your Turn 2

> In this passage, there are capitalization errors. See how many you can find.

the mayor of our city, warren grimmes, will be the speaker at a dinner for tony winslow. mr. winslow will be given the farwell city man of the year award. mr. winslow rescued three people from a burning house last december.

a member of governor findlay's staff will be there to honor mr. winslow, too. the entire winslow family will be present. two hundred people are expected at farwell high school for the ceremony. my sister cathy and i will be there because mr. winslow's daughter betty is a good friend of ours. our mother and father are planning to go, too. it should be a night to remember in farwell.

Once you have learned the rules of capitalization, you will find that it is not too difficult to know what letters to capitalize. Remember that the first letter of names and places is capitalized. You will be able to handle most common capitalization problems.

Punctuation

The most common punctuation errors occur when a period is used after a group of words that do not form a complete sentence. **This is called a sentence fragment.** A sentence fragment occurs when you do not include a *subject* or a *verb* in a sentence.

An example of a sentence fragment that does not contain a subject is:

Walking down the street in a great hurry.

In this sentence fragment, we do not know who is walking down the street. There is no subject.

BETTER: Charlie was walking down the street in a great hurry.

An example of a sentence fragment that does not contain a verb is:

Rachel slowly and quietly down the path in the sunlight.

In this sentence fragment, there is no verb to tell us what Rachel was doing.

BETTER: Rachel walked slowly and quietly down the path in the sunlight.

How do you know if you have a complete sentence? Ask yourself:

★ *Do I know who or what the sentence is about?*

      If you do, then the sentence has a subject.

★ *Do I know what the subject is doing?*

      If you do, then the sentence has a verb.

If you have a subject, a verb, and a complete thought then you have a sentence. You should know what or who the sentence is about and what is happening.

To help you decide if a group of words is a sentence, think of two high walls. One wall is at the beginning of the group of words. The other wall is at the end of the words. You should be able to read just the words between these two walls and know **who or what the sentence is about** (the subject). You should also know **what the subject is doing** (the verb). If you know these things, then you have a sentence, not a sentence fragment.

In addition to verbs that show action, there are verbs that are used to show a "state of being." These are words such as: **is, are, was, were, have been**, or **will be**. Think of these types of verbs as the "glue" that holds ideas together. They help sentences make sense.

An example of this might be:

> Willie is worried about his grade.

★ We can see that "Willie" is the subject. The sentence is about Willie.
★ "Worried" is how Willie feels.
★ Connecting the subject (*Willie*) to how Willie feels (*worried*) is the word **is**. **Is** is the verb. It makes the idea whole. *State of being verbs* act in this way – like *connectors* between parts of a sentence.

By checking for subjects and verbs, you may notice that you have used periods to make a sentence when you do not really have a complete sentence.

✍ Your Turn 3

➤ Below are some sentence fragments. Change them into complete sentences by adding subjects and/or verbs.

1. Johanna, a very good dancer.

2. Wandering down the peaceful country road whistling a happy tune.

3. Singing popular songs in the shower.

4. Sometimes, the birds at the snow-covered feeder.

5. Bluejays, very active birds.

6. At the height of his popularity.

Another very common error is connecting two ideas that would be clearer if they were separate. These kind of sentences are called "run-on" sentences. The idea *runs on* for too long. They happen when two or more parts of the sentence are joined with the word "and." Before you know it, you have a long sentence. Punctuation can solve this problem. You can put a comma before the "and" or make the ideas two separate sentences by using a period.

Whether a comma or a period is used is often up to you. Remember we must separate the ideas. This will make your writing clearer. Let's look at some examples of how this punctuation error can be corrected.

> The family parked the car and then they took the picnic things out of the car and walked to the park.

This run-on sentence could be revised in a number of ways. Here are two:

1
> The family parked the car. Then, they took the picnic things out of the car and walked to the park.

2
> The family parked the car. Then, they took the picnic things out of the car. Finally, they walked to the park.

Look at the second example. Notice how the signal words we used in Chapter Four can make separating sentences easier. They can help you make your writing clearer.

✍ Your Turn 4

> In the examples given below, decide how you can correct the run-on sentences.

1. Terry went to the bank to cash a check and he went to the mall to buy a new pair of jeans.

2. The mail arrived at eleven o'clock and Patty went to the mail box and she took the mail into the house.

3. Whitney liked to lip sync the songs she heard on the tapes she thought she could become a better singer that way.

4. While waiting for the bus to take him to the mall, Shawn decided to check his wallet to see how much money he had and he found that he had only twenty dollars in his wallet.

5. First, Chuck called his friend Willand then he called his friend Nick and they agreed to meet on the basketball court at ten o'clock for a practice shooting session.

Types of Punctuation Problems

Writers do not make many punctuation errors at the end of sentences. They know that most sentences end with a period, a question mark, or an exclamation mark. Most errors usually involve commas.

Part of the problem is that commas have so many different uses. There are at least eleven different times when a comma may be the proper punctuation to use. Beginning writers may have problems with correctly using commas for all purposes. We will learn some of the most common uses for a comma.

The Comma

A comma is usually used after a signal word. Some common signal words are **therefore, however, moreover, later, finally, so, first,** and **but**. When you see these kinds of words at the beginning of a sentence, you may need a comma.

> Bill wanted to go to the park. **However**, he had too much homework.

Sometimes, the signals used to link the ideas from one sentence to another will be a phrase rather than a single word. These include **in other words, in addition,** or **on the other hand**. You can see how these words or phrases grab your attention. They prepare you to read additional information about a topic or an opposite view on a topic. That is why a comma is needed. It allows you to pause before continuing to read.

✎ Your Turn 5

● ●

> ➤ Decide where a comma should be used to separate a signal word or phrase from the rest of the sentence.

1. However the rest of the chorus was prepared to sing the three songs on the program.

2. Soon afterwards the band was tuning up for the program.

3. But the two groups needed to come together to perform the concert.

4. In addition the audience expected to hear the entire concert during the rehearsal.

5. On the other hand the rehearsal audience cannot expect to hear the program at its best.

6. Therefore the audience is warned that the performance may not be complete.

A comma is also used when a sentence is introduced by a phrase. When this occurs, the comma is used to separate the phrase from the rest of the sentence.

At the store, Gina bought milk, eggs, and cheese.

✍ Your Turn 6

• •

➤ These sentences contain phrases that need to be separated from the rest of the sentence by commas.

1. Walking on the beach the family stopped to look at the shells that they saw.

2. In the mall the boys went to the store to look for the jeans they liked to wear.

3. Not for the first time Sharon wondered if she should begin her skiing now or later.

4. Above the bank the sign flashed the time, the date, and the temperature.

5. With a sigh of relief the tennis team learned that they had made the finals.

When a sentence contains some extra information, a comma is needed to separate it from the sentence. An example would be the following:

Caitlin, a very promising gymnast, entered the contest.

Other examples would be:

> The teacher, Mr. Carnegie, is going away on vacation.

> Tania, a member of the student council, is a very good friend of mine.

How can you decide if some information is helpful, but not needed? You should block out those words and see if you understand the sentence without that group of words.

Read the sentence about the teacher. Block out the part between the commas. Is the main idea of the sentence still easy to understand? If you did not know the teacher's name, you would still be able to understand the sentence. It is helpful to have the teacher's name, but it is not necessary to the meaning of the sentence.

In the sentence about Tania, the important point of the sentence is that Tania is the writer's friend. She may also be a member of the student council, but this is not the main point. Because this information is less important, it is separated by commas.

✐ Your Turn 7

> Add commas to separate the extra information from the rest of the sentence.

1. Bailey a very tall sophomore is a player for the high school basketball team.

2. Diana the president of the student council is active in a school club that helps senior citizens.

3. Ms. Densey the manager of our local Burger King has been most helpful in our fund-raising effort.

Another important use of the comma is to separate two parts of a sentence joined by a **conjunction**. Conjunctions are words such as: **and**, **but**, and **or**. The most common conjunction is the word **and**. To join two complete sentences together with the word "and," we need to use a comma before the "and."

Look at this example:

> Ellen waited for almost twenty minutes
> for her friend Gina, and Gina never came.

The two parts of this sentence joined by "and" are complete sentences. There is a subject and a verb (*Ellen waited*) before the "and." There is another subject and verb (*Gina came*) after the "and." Therefore, a comma is needed in order to separate the two parts of the sentence. A comma would be placed before the "and." Separating the sentences by using a period is also possible. But if you choose to keep the ideas together, you must use a comma before the "and."

✍ Your Turn 8

● ●

> ➤ In this exercise, place commas where two complete sentences are joined with a conjunction.

1. Mario took first place in his race at the track meet and his team ranked second after two events.

2. Cindy tried to pack all of her clothes into one suitcase but she could not fit her shoes into the case.

3. Mr. Chan said that the whole family might go to San Francisco for their vacation or they could go to the Grand Canyon.

4. The school musical will be presented in late March and the rehearsals will begin by mid-January.

5. He thought he did well on his math test but his score was not as high as he thought it would be.

The comma is also used to separate things that are in a series. You need to remember to use a comma to separate three or more items when they appear in a sentence. An example would be:

> Ellen needed to take her glove, her bat, and her baseball cap to practice.

It is quite common for writers to forget to put the commas between things that are listed in a series.

✍ Your Turn 9

> In these sentences, put the commas where they are needed to separate the items in a series.

1. On Saturday, Frank went to the mall to the movies and to a friend's house.

2. Gene had grown so much that he couldn't wear his shirts his jeans his jacket or his sneakers.

3. Liz Karen and Melissa walked home together everyday after school.

4. Dee knew that she would need wire a battery a lightbulb and a switch for her science project.

5. This year the family decided to plant tomatoes lettuce string beans and peas in their garden.

As we stated earlier, there are many times when we need to use commas in our writing. We have discussed some of those times. There is one more time when a comma is important. That is when we are including quotations in our writing.

Quotation Marks

Quotation marks are a writer's way of showing the reader the exact words someone says. Writers need to remember three things when you use quotation marks.

1. If you include anything in the sentence that is not part of the quotation, it has to be separated from the quotation by a comma.

2. The first word of the quotation must begin with a capital letter.

3. The quotation marks almost always come *after* the end punctuation of a sentence.

Let's look at some examples of quotations and see how they are punctuated.

Example 1

> Harry's mother said, "Don't forget to come right home after school."

In this sentence, we have to separate who is speaking, Harry's mother, from the exact words she said. We do this by using a comma after the word **said**. The first letter of the word she spoke is written with a capital letter, and the entire sentence she spoke is inside the quotation marks. The period is also placed inside the quotation marks.

Example 2

> "I want to be the first one there," said
> Yvette.

In this example, the quotation appears first. The comma follows the last word of the quotation and appears *before* **said**. The comma should always appear before the end quotation marks. If the quotation were a question or an exclamation, you would not need the comma. Look at this example:

> "Do you want to go with me to the
> movies?" asked Jennifer.

Here is a strategy to use when writing sentences that have quotations. Think about quotation marks by imagining that you are catching a ball. Your two hands fit around the ball. Quotation marks are used to "catch the words." They fit around the words, like your hands fit around the ball.

✍ Your Turn 10
• •

> ➤ In the following sentences, put in the quotation marks, capitals and the commas that are needed.

1. Mr. Drucker asked does anyone have any questions about what will be on the history quiz?

2. Debbie asked her friends are any of you going to the party at Scott's house?

3. Ron and Trish are planning to go said Keith.

4. David replied I wanted to go, but I have to baby-sit for a neighbor that night.

The Apostrophe

The **apostrophe** is another punctuation mark that you should know how to use. The apostrophe is used in two special cases.

The first use of an apostrophe is to show when someone owns something. This is called a **possessive**. The apostrophe is always used with an "s." An example of a possessive is:

Aaron's cat greeted me at the door.

The second use of an apostrophe is in a **contraction**. A contraction is the putting together of two words. Examples of contractions are **don't**, **shouldn't**, **isn't**, and **haven't**. Each of these contractions is a verb with *not* added to the end.

don't = do not

shouldn't = should not

isn't = is not

haven't = have not

The apostrophe is used to fill in for the missing letters. Contractions are not correct if they lack apostrophes.

Summary

In this chapter, we have looked at some of the things writers do to improve their written work. They check:

★ their spelling

★ their capitalization

★ their punctuation

Soon, you will get used to checking for these three important things. As you write, you may even begin to fix things without thinking about it.

There may be other kinds of corrections you need to make in your writing. You will learn how to make some of these changes as you do the exercises in the next chapter. You will also get to practice the skills you learned in this chapter.

UNIT 4: Practicing Editing and Revising Skills

CHAPTER SIX: SELECTION 1 – MODELED INSTRUCTION

We have shown you some ways you can revise and edit your writing. We have given you the chance to practice these skills. Now, you will have the chance to practice them in a test format.

You will be given writing passages to read. After each passage are multiple-choice questions. The questions are about revising and editing the written text.

We will help you answer the questions after the first piece of writing. After the multiple-choice questions, we show you which answers are correct and why.

We will guide you through the answering process after the second piece of writing. After each multiple-choice question, you will need to explain why you chose the answer you did. This will guide your work on future tests.

You will have the chance to practice what you have learned with the third piece of writing. After the writing, answer the multiple-choice questions just as if you were taking a test.

This first piece of practice writing is a letter of complaint about a product. At the end of the letter there are nine multiple-choice questions to answer. The questions are about common revising and editing problems. First, choose the answers that you think are correct. We have modeled the thinking you should do when you answer multiple-choice questions. Read the answers after the questions to find out which choice is best and why. Make sure to read why the wrong answers are not correct.

Introduction

Juan and his wife bought a television at a local department store. A few weeks after they brought it home, there was a storm. During the storm, the television was destroyed by lightning. Juan and his wife took the television back to the department store. They wanted to replace it. But, the clerk who sold them the television would not replace it. So, Juan decided to write a letter to the store's owner.

4046 Boulevard East
South Meadow, NY 12345
October 24, 199_

Mr. Robert Overletter
Outstanding Department Store
46 Main Street
South Meadow, NY 12345

Dear Mr. Overletter:

1 I am writing to ask for a new television set. The television we bought in your Store was destroyed by lightning.

2 Three weeks ago, my wife and I bought a television for our living room. One of your salespeople tolled us it could be played anytime. He said an electrical storm would not harm the television. It had a special part that protected it from lightning.

3 Last Friday, we had a big storm and lightning struck the area. I asked my wife if I should turn off the television. She said no. After all, it has something to protect it from lightning. Later, I heard a loud crack. My television went dark. I pulled the plug from the wall. But, the damage had been done.

4 We packed up the television and we went back to the store. When we told the salesperson about the problem, he said it wasn't the store's fault. I told him that he had said there was something in the television that protected it from lightning. He said we were misstaken. He told us that he never said that. My wife said she heard him say it, too.

5 I am asking you to replace the television. The reason we bought it was because it had protection from lightning. Now, we find the salesperson lied to us.

6 Thank you for taking care of this matter.

Yours truly,

Juan Morales

1. What editing change, if any, would you make in the second sentence of paragraph 1 *("The television we bought in your Store was destroyed by lightning.")*?

    A. Change **television** to **telvision.**

    B. Change **Store** to **store.**

    C. Add a comma after **television.**

    D. Make no change.

2. What editing change, if any, would you make in the first sentence of paragraph 2 *("Three weeks ago, my wife and I bought a television for our living room.")*?

    A. Omit the comma after **ago.**

    B. Change **weeks** to **week's.**

    C. Change **wife** to **Wife.**

    D. Make no change.

3. What editing change, if any, would you make in the second sentence of paragraph 2 *("One of your salespeople tolled us it could be played anytime.")*?

    A. Change **salespeople** to **Salespeople.**

    B. Change **tolled** to **told.**

    C. Add a period after **salespeople.**

    D. Make no change.

4. What editing change, if any, would you make in the first sentence of paragraph 3 *("Last Friday, we had a big storm and lightning struck the area.")*?

    A. Add a comma after **storm.**

    B. Add a comma after **and.**

    C. Change **struck** to **strucke.**

    D. Make no change.

5. How would you make the third and fourth sentences in paragraph 3 into a direct quote (*"She said no. After all, it has something to protect it from lightning."*)?

    A. She said "no." "After all, it has something to protect it from lightning."

    B. She said "no after all it has something to protect it from lightning."

    C. She said, "No. After all, it has something to protect it from lightning."

    D. She said, "No. "After all it has something to protect it from lightning."

6. What editing change, if any, would you make in the first sentence of paragraph 4 (*"We packed up the television and we went back to the store."*)?

    A. Add a comma after **television.**

    B. Add a comma after **and**.

    C. Change the second **we** to **We.**

    D. Make no change.

7. What editing change, if any, would you make in the fourth sentence of paragraph 4 (*"He said we were misstaken."*)?

    A. Add a comma after **said.**

    B. Add quotation marks before **We** and after **misstaken.**

    C. Change **misstaken** to **mistaken.**

    D. Make no change.

8. Where would be the best place to move the last sentence of paragraph 4 (*"My wife said she heard him say it, too."*)?

    A. to paragraph 3 right after the sentence, "After all, it has something to protect it from lightning."

    B. to paragraph 3 right after the sentence, "I pulled the plug from the wall."

    C. to paragraph 4 right after the sentence, "We packed up the television and we went back to the store."

    D. to paragraph 4 right after the sentence, "I told him that he had said there was something in the television that protected it from lightning."

9. What does the word **struck** mean in the first sentence of paragraph 3 (*"Last Friday, we had a big storm and lightning struck the area."*)?

    A. outstanding

    B. hit

    C. unusual

    D. turned to

Modeled Instruction: Correct Answers

Question 1

Hint: To decide on the correct answer, review the following editing skills: capitalization, contractions, and punctuation. After you review what you know about each of these, you will be better able to make the correct choice.

Choice A is not correct. **Television** is spelled correctly.

Choice B is correct. The first letter of **store** should not be capitalized. This is not a proper noun. Juan does not identify the store by name. If he had written **Outstanding Department Store**, then the "s" would need to be capitalized.

Choice C is not correct. A comma is not needed in this sentence.

Choice D is not correct. One of the first three choices contains a correct answer.

Question 2

Hint: To decide on the correct answer, you need to use what you know about commas, possessives, and capitalization.

Choice A is not correct. You need the comma in this sentence. **Three weeks ago** is a phrase. It introduces the sentence. This means that you need a comma to separate these words from the rest of the sentence.

Choice B is not correct. You need the plural form of the word **week**, because Juan wrote *Three* **weeks**. The week doesn't own anything. So, you would not use the possessive, which is **week's**.

Choice C is not correct. The word **wife** is not a name. It is not a proper noun. It should not be capitalized.

Choice D is correct. None of the other choices is a correct answer.

Question 3

Choice A is not correct. The word **salespeople** should not be capitalized. It is not a proper noun. It is not being used as a person's name.

Choice B is the correct answer. The word **tolled** is spelled incorrectly. **Told** is the correct spelling.

Choice C is not correct. **One of your salespeople** is a phrase. It is not a complete sentence because it does not contain a verb.

Choice D is not correct. One of the first three choices contains a correct answer.

Question 4

Choice A is correct. The sentence really contains two separate ideas that are joined by the conjunction **and**. Therefore, a comma is needed to separate these two independent thoughts.

Choice B is not correct. When separating two complete sentences, the comma goes before, not after, the conjunction.

Choice C is not correct. **Struck**, the past tense of the verb **strike**, is spelled correctly.

Choice D is not correct. One of the first three choices contains a correct answer.

Question 5

Hint: This is a revision question. You need to consider how some of the material in the selection might best be rewritten.

Choice A is not correct. You do not put quotation marks around every sentence someone speaks if the sentences are written one right after the other.

Choice B is not correct. The "N" in **no** needs to be capitalized because it is the first word Juan's wife said.

Choice C is correct. The quotation marks have been correctly placed at the beginning and end of the quote. Also, a comma was placed after **said**.

Choice D is not correct. The quotation mark before **After** is not necessary.

Question 6

Choice A is correct. When using a comma to separate two complete sentences, it goes before the conjunction.

Choice B is not correct. When using a comma to separate two complete sentences, it goes before the conjunction, not after it.

Choice C is not correct. The second **We** is not a proper noun. It should not be capitalized.

Choice D is not correct. One of the first three choices contains a correct answer.

Question 7

Choice A is not correct. There is no need to put a comma after **said** because there is not a direct quote in this sentence.

Choice B is not correct. This sentence does not contain the exact words the salesperson said. He would not have said, "*We* were mistaken." Therefore, there should not be quotation marks around those words.

Choice C is correct. The word **misstaken** is spelled incorrectly. **Mistaken** is the correct spelling.

Choice D is not correct. One of the first three choices contains a correct answer.

Question 8

Hint: To decide if there is a better place for this sentence, read the sentence in the places suggested in each choice. This will help you to decide where it should be placed.

Choice A is not correct. The sentence does not make sense here: "After all, it has something to protect it from lightning. My wife said she heard him say it, too."

Choice B is not correct. The sentence does not make sense here: "I pulled the plug from the wall. My wife said she heard him say it, too."

Choice C is not correct. The sentence does not make sense here: "We packed up the television and we went back to the store. My wife said she heard him say it, too."

Choice D is correct. Both sentences mention what the salesperson said. They should come right after each other.

Question 9

Hint: This is a vocabulary question. You need to decide which meaning of the word is correct here.

Choice A is not correct. **Struck** is the past tense of the verb **strike**. **Outstanding** is an adjective.

Choice B is correct. In this text, the word **struck** means **hit**. Both words are verbs, and one can replace the other. "Lightning *hit* the area."

Choice C is not correct. **Unusual** is an adjective.

Choice D is not correct. "Turned to" is a verb. But, that is not the meaning in this sentence. "Lightning *turned to* the area" does not make sense.

CHAPTER SEVEN: SELECTION 2 – GUIDED INSTRUCTION

The second piece of writing is also a letter of complaint. At the end of the letter, there are eight multiple-choice questions to answer. You will need to use common revising and editing skills. First, choose the answer for each question that you think is correct. Write why you think it is the best possible answer. Then think about why the other choices are not correct. Your teacher has the correct answers. Discuss your answers with your teacher or another student.

219 Rolling Hills Road
Carlisle, PA 12345
September 21, 199_

Mountain Bike Inc.
35 West Main Street
Chicago, IL 12345

Dear Sir:

1 Last week I bought a mountain bike at the local bike store. I used money from my paper route to buy this bike. The bike came in three parts and had to be put together. I had never put a mountain bike together. So, the clerk agreed to assemble the parts.

2 I rode the bike home, and everything worked fine. The next day, my best friend and I went rideing on dirt-bike trails. Everything worked well for the first 30 minutes. Then, I felt the chain slipping. I shifted gears, and it stopped.

3 On the way home from the trails, I stopped in the bike store. The clerk looked at the bike. He noticed one sprocket had broken off. It had broken off the large sprocket wheel. He said I had broken it when I was shifting gears. I told him that I never had a sprocket wheel brake on a bike before. He told me I would need to pay for a new large sprocket wheel.

4 I am writing to ask for a new large sprocket wheel. The one I got with my bike is defective. It should not have broken so easily. I have owned this bike for only two days. If a sprocket wheel breaks after only two days of riding something is very wrong.

5 I would like to receive a new sprocket wheel as soon as possible. It is part #19643. Thank you.

Yours truly,

Jamie Baxter
Jamie Baxter

1. What editing change, if any, would you make in the first sentence of paragraph 1 (*"Last week I bought a mountain bike at the local bike store."*)?

    A. Add a comma after **week.**

    B. Change **mountain bike** to **Mountain Bike.**

    C. Change **bike store** to **Bike Store.**

    D. Make no change.

The answer is _____.

Reason for choice _____

_____

☞ *Think about why the other choices are not correct.*

2. What transition word is needed at the beginning of the fourth sentence of paragraph 1 (*"I had never put a mountain bike together."*)?

    A. Finally,

    B. But,

    C. First,

    D. Later,

The answer is _____.

Reason for choice _____

_____

☞ *Think about why the other choices are not correct.*

3. What editing change, if any, would you make in the second sentence of paragraph 2 (*"The next day, my best friend and I went rideing on dirt-bike trails."*)?

    A. Change **friend** to **freind**.

    B. Delete the comma after **day**.

    C. Change **rideing** to **riding**.

    D. Change **trails** to **trailes**.

The answer is _____.

Reason for choice _____

_____

    ☞ *Think about why the other choices are not correct.*

4. What is the best way to combine the third and fourth sentences of paragraph 3 (*"He noticed one sprocket had broken off. It had broken off the large sprocket wheel."*)?

    A. He noticed one sprocket had broken off it had broken off the large sprocket wheel.

    B. He noticed one sprocket and it had broken off the large sprocket wheel.

    C. He noticed one sprocket had broken off the large sprocket wheel.

    D. He noticed one sprocket had broken off but it had broken off the large sprocket wheel.

The answer is _____.

Reason for choice _____

_____

    ☞ *Think about why the other choices are not correct.*

5. What editing change, if any, would you make in the sixth sentence of paragraph 3 (*"I told him that I never had a sprocket wheel brake on a bike before."*)?

    A. Change **brake** to **break.**

    B. Change **before** to **befor.**

    C. Change **had** to **have.**

    D. Make no change.

The answer is _____.

Reason for choice _____

_____

☞ *Think about why the other choices are not correct.*

6. What does the word "**defective**" mean in the second sentence of paragraph 4 (*"The one I got with my bike is defective."*)?

    A. a person who searches for clues

    B. perfect

    C. ugly

    D. not the way it should be

The answer is _____.

Reason for choice _____

_____

☞ *Think about why the other choices are not correct.*

7. What editing change, if any, would you make in the fifth sentence of paragraph 4 (*"If a sprocket wheel breaks after only two days of riding something is very wrong."*)?

    A. Change **breaks** to **break's.**

    B. Add a comma after **riding.**

    C. Change **something** to **some thing.**

    D. Change **wrong** to **rong.**

The answer is _____.

Reason for choice _____

_____

☞ *Think about why the other choices are not correct.*

8. Which sentence does not add anything to the main idea of the letter?

    A. "I used money from my paper route to buy this bike."

    B. "I shifted gears, and it stopped."

    C. "He noticed one sprocket had broken off."

    D. "I am writing to ask for a new large sprocket wheel."

The answer is _____.

Reason for choice _____

_____

☞ *Think about why the other choices are not correct.*

CHAPTER EIGHT: SELECTION 3 – INDEPENDENT PRACTICE

The third piece of writing is a friendly letter. This one asks for advice. At the end of the letter, there are six multiple-choice questions to answer. The questions are about common revising and editing problems. Choose the answers that you think are correct. Your teacher has the correct answers. Discuss your answers with your teacher or another student.

71 Decatur Boulevard
Merryville, GA 12345
April 2, 199_

Dear Faith,

1   I need your help. My best friend and i tried out to be cheerleaders. I made it, and she didn't. Now she wont talk to me anymore. Every time I see her in school, she turns the other way.

2   We have been friend's ever since I moved into my house. She lives only three houses away, and I always stopped at her house on the way to school. We walked to school together. Now, she leaves for school early to avoid me.

3   The other day I tried to talk to her. I told her I was sorry she didn't make the cheerleading squad. I told her I wished that she could have been picked with me and the other girls. I even said she was a better cheerleader than I am. She said thanks and walked away. I asked her what was wrong. She turned to me and said it had nothing to do with me. She was upset she hadn't made the squad. It meant we wouldn't be together in the fall. That is when I would be at the games with the other cheerleaders. She thanked me for trying to help.

4   I can understand that she is unhappy, but why is she angry with me. The coach picked the squad. I didn't pick it. What does she want me to do?

5   Please give me some advice on how I can get my friend back.

Sincerely,

Amy

1. What editing change, if any, would you make in the second sentence of paragraph 1 (*"My best friend and i tried out to be cheerleaders."*)?

    A. Add a comma after **friend.**

    B. Add a comma after **i.**

    C. Change **i** to **I.**

    D. Make no change.

2. What editing change, if any, would you make in the fourth sentence of paragraph 1 (*"Now she wont talk to me anymore."*)?

    A. Change **anymore** to **no more.**

    B. Add a comma after **talk.**

    C. Change **wont** to **won't.**

    D. Make no change.

3. What editing change, if any, would you make in the first sentence in paragraph 2 (*"We have been friend's ever since I moved into my house."*)?

    A. Change **have** to **has.**

    B. Change **friend's** to **friends.**

    C. Add a comma after **friend's.**

    D. Make no change.

4. What does the word **squad** mean in the second sentence of paragraph 3 (*"I told her I was sorry she didn't make the cheerleading squad."*)?

    A. girls

    B. fish

    C. team

    D. police

5. What is the best way to shorten the run-on sentence in paragraph 2 (*"She lives only three houses away, and I always stopped at her house on the way to school"*)?

    A. She lives only three houses away. I always stopped at her house. On the way to school.

    B. She lives only three houses away. I always stopped at her house on the way to school.

    C. She lives. Only three houses away. I always stopped at her house on the way to school.

    D. She lives only three houses away, I always stopped at her house on the way to school.

6. What editing change, if any, would you make in the first sentence of paragraph 4 (*"I can understand that she is unhappy, but why is she angry with me."*)?

    A. Change the period to a question mark.

    B. Change **unhappy** to **unhapy.**

    C. Change **angry** to **angrey.**

    D. Make no change.

UNIT 5: Practice Writing Tests

CHAPTER NINE: PRACTICE TESTS

In this chapter, you will practice what you have learned by taking two model tests.

On the first part of each test, you will be given a topic to write about. Before you begin writing, use a prewriting strategy that you think you will help you organize your ideas. This will help you decide what you want to write. Then, think of a good beginning paragraph and a good ending paragraph. The paragraphs in between will have the different ideas you planned in your prewriting strategy.

On the second part of each test, you will read a passage. Then you have to answer multiple-choice questions using your editing and revising skills. Before answering any of the questions, think about the different choices. Reread the section of the writing that the question is about. See how each of the choices would or would not correct the problem. You will need to think about spelling, capitalization, punctuation, and other skills you have learned. Select the choice that seems to improve the piece of writing in the best way.

TEST A: Part 1

This is a chance to show how well you can write. You will be asked to write an essay on a topic. Your writing will be judged on how well you keep to the topic, how well you organize your ideas, and how well you edit what you have written.

> ❯ Read the writing task below.

> ❯ Take time to think about what you wish to say.

> ❯ Use a prewriting strategy. Put down your ideas before you begin your draft.

> ❯ Write a first draft.

> ❯ When you have finished writing, read your essay to see if you want to make any revisions.

> ❯ Review your essay carefully to see if you want to make any editing changes.

> ❯ Make the revisions and editing changes you need to make.

Writing Task

You have heard some of your friends at work making fun of a new employee. This bothers you. You decide to write a letter for the company newsletter about this situation.

Your letter might be about being kind to people, or it might be about how we can hurt people with unkind remarks. Give details or examples to support how you feel.

Nick has written this essay to post on the school bulletin board. He has asked you to review the essay before he posts it. What editing changes would you recommend?

Should Students Look Like Clones?

1   Last week at a school-board meeting a new board member said that starting in the fall, students should wear uniforms. Wearing uniforms in school is not new. There are schools in our country that do this. There is a reason for doing this. Uniforms stop problems between student who can buy clothes that cost a lot and those who can't.

2   This isn't why the board member suggested we wear uniforms. He just dont like the clothes some of us wear. He wants everyone to look alike. It wood make us clones.

3   I think this is wrong. This board member isn't saying that our clothes are dangerous or causing a problem. He just doesn't like some of the popular styles of today.

4   Sometimes, my parents and i don't agree on things such as clothes. Then we talk about the problem and decide what to do about it. They understand that it is important for me to be me. They understand that sometimes I like to wear what is popular and I like to look like everyone else. However, there are times when I want to look different.

5   My parents say this is all part of growing up. I don't think that wearing uniforms will help us to become more better people. How could making everyone look like clones be good. I am against wearing uniforms in school.

1. What editing change, if any, would you make in the first sentence of paragraph 1 (*"Last week at a school-board meeting a new board member said that starting in the fall, students should wear uniforms."*)?

    A. Add commas after **week** and **meeting.**

    B. Change **fall** to **Fall.**

    C. Change **students** to **student's.**

    D. Make no change.

2. What editing change, if any, would you make in the second sentence of paragraph 1 (*"Wearing uniforms in school is not new."*)?

    A. Change **not** to **no.**

    B. Change **is** to **are.**

    C. Change **new** to **knew.**

    D. Make no change.

3. What editing change, if any, would you make in the third sentence of paragraph 1 (*"There are schools in our country that do this."*)?

    A. Change **There** to **Their.**

    B. Change **country** to **Country.**

    C. Add a comma after **country.**

    D. Make no change.

4. What editing change, if any, would you make in the fifth sentence of paragraph 1 (*"Uniforms stop problems between student who can buy clothes that cost a lot and those who can't."*)?

    A. Change **student** to **students.**

    B. Add a comma after **clothes.**

    C. Change **can't** to **cann't.**

    D. Make no change.

5. What editing change, if any, would you make in the second sentence of paragraph 2 *("He just dont like the clothes some of us wear.")*?

      A. Change **dont** to **don't.**
      B. Change **dont** to **doesn't.**
      C. Change **wear** to **ware.**
      D. Make no change.

6. What editing change, if any, would you make in the last sentence of paragraph 2 *("It wood make us clones.")*?

      A. Change **wood** to **would.**
      B. Change **us** to **Us.**
      C. Add a comma after **wood.**
      D. Make no change.

7. What editing change, if any, would you make in the first sentence of paragraph 4 *("Sometimes, my parents and i don't agree on things such as clothes.")*?

      A. Change **Sometimes** to **Some times.**
      B. Delete the comma after **Sometimes.**
      C. Change **i** to **I.**
      D. Make no change.

8. What editing change, if any, would you make in the fourth sentence of paragraph 4 *("They understand that sometimes I like to wear what is popular and I like to look like everyone else.")*?

      A. Add a comma after **sometimes**.
      B. Add a comma after **popular.**
      C. Add a comma after **and**.
      D. Make no change.

9. What editing change, if any, would you make in the second sentence of paragraph 5 (*"I don't think that wearing uniforms will help us to become more better people."*)?

    A. Add a comma after **think.**

    B. Add a comma after **uniforms.**

    C. Delete **more.**

    D. Make no change.

10. What editing change, if any, would you make in the third sentence of paragraph 5 (*"How could making everyone look like clones be good."*)?

    A. Add a comma after **How.**

    B. Add a comma after **clones.**

    C. Change the period to a question mark.

    D. Make no change.

TEST B: Part 1

This is a chance to show how well you can write. You will be asked to write an essay on a topic. Your writing will be judged on how well you keep to the topic, how well you organize your ideas, and how well you edit what you have written.

> ❯ Read the writing task below.

> ❯ Take time to think about what you wish to say.

> ❯ Use a prewriting strategy. Put down your ideas before you begin your draft.

> ❯ Write a first draft.

> ❯ When you have finished writing, read your essay to see if you want to make any revisions.

> ❯ Review your essay carefully to see if you want to make any editing changes.

> ❯ Make the revisions and editing changes you need to make.

Writing Task

Write a review of a movie, a book, or a television program. In your review, give important information about the plot, setting, and characters. If you liked it, tell your reasons for liking it. If you did not like it, explain why not.

Sharon has written this letter to her friend Amelia. She has asked you to review the letter before she mails it. What editing changes would you recommend?

12 Candlewick Avenue
Woodsmen, OH 12345
August 25, 199_

Dear Amelia,

1 I need your advice. My sister is moving back home. She is five years older than I am. She lost her job and she cannot pay the rent for her apartment.

2 When she went away, I moved in to her room. It is bigger than my old room and it has a window with a nice view. My sister said I could have it. No one expected her to live at home again.

3 Now, my sister wants to move back into her old room. My parents say I should move to my old room. They say my sister is upset about losing her job and giving her back her old room will make her feel better.

4 I know that my sister is upset. I think what my parints want me to do is wrong. Ive spent money to decorate the room. I painted the walls a light blue. My sister and I don't like the same colors. I bought curtains and a bedspread to match the walls. I bought a lamp to put next to my bed. The room is just the way I like it. It isn't fare that I have to give up the room after I have done all this work.

5 How can I get my parents to let me keep my room? I think it is unfair to make me give up my room. Because she is coming back.

6 Write soon. My sister is coming home in three weeks.

Sincerely,

Sharon

1. What editing change, if any, would you make in the last sentence of paragraph 1 *("She lost her job and she cannot pay the rent for her apartment.")*?

    A. Change **lost** to **lossed.**
    B. Add a comma after **job.**
    C. Add a comma after **rent.**
    D. Make no change.

2. What editing change, if any, would you make in the first sentence of paragraph 2 *("When she went away, I moved in to her room.")*?

    A. Change **went** to **gone.**
    B. Delete the comma after **away.**
    C. Change **in to** to **into.**
    D. Make no change.

3. What editing change, if any, would you make in the second sentence of paragraph 2 *("It is bigger than my old room and it has a window with a nice view.")*?

    A. Change **bigger** to **biger.**
    B. Add a comma after **room.**
    C. Change **it has** to **it's**.
    D. Make no change.

4. What editing change, if any, would you make in the second sentence of paragraph 4 *("I think what my parints want me to do is wrong.")*?

    A. Add a comma after **parints**.
    B. Change **parints** to **parents.**
    C. Change **wrong** to **rong**.
    D. Make no change.

5. What editing change, if any, would you make in the third sentence of paragraph 4 (*"Ive spent money to decorate the room."*)?

      A. Change **Ive** to **I've.**

      B. Add a comma after **spent** and **money.**

      C. Change **spent** to **spend.**

      D. Make no change.

6. What editing change, if any, would you make in the last sentence of paragraph 4 (*"It isn't fare that I have to give up the room after I have done all this work."*)?

      A. Change **isn't** to **don't.**

      B. Change **fare** to **fair.**

      C. Change **done** to **did.**

      D. Make no change.

7. What is the best way to combine the last two sentences in paragraph 5 (*"I think it is unfair to make me give up my room. Because she is coming back."*)?

      A. I think it is unfair to make me give up my room because she is coming back.

      B. I think it is unfair to make me give up my room, but because she is coming back.

      C. I think it is unfair, to make me give up my room, because she is coming back.

      D. I think it is unfair to make me give up my room, because she is coming back.

8. Which sentence does not add anything to the main idea of the letter?

      A. My sister is moving back home.

      B. No one expected her to live at home again.

      C. I think what my parints want me to do is wrong.

      D. My sister and I don't like the same colors.